OPENERS

OPENERS

by Amy Nathan
Photographs by Kathryn Kleinman
Styling by Amy Nathan
Text by Jo Mancuso
Book design by Jacqueline Jones

Chronicle Books San Francisco

Library of Congress Cataloging in Publication Data:
  Nathan, Amy.
  Openers/by Amy Nathan; photographs by Kathryn Kleinman.
     p.   cm.
  Includes index.
   ISBN 0-87701-512-0 ISBN 0-87701-449-3 (pbk.):
   1. Cookery (Appetizers) I. Kleinman, Kathryn. II. Title.
TX740.N365 1988   88-2908
641.8′12 — dc19   CIP

Art direction by Amy Nathan and Kathryn Kleinman
Recipe and food assistance by Bob Lambert and
Stephanie Greenleigh
Edited by Carolyn Miller
Photography assistance by Lisa Osta
Mechanical production by Suzanne Hidekawa, Suzanne
Skugstad, and Ignatius Tanzil, Jacqueline Jones Design
Calligraphy by William Stewart

Page 11: From "Social Studies" included in "Knee Plays"
by David Byrne and Robert Wilson
Copyright 1985
Reprinted with Permission

Distributed in Canada by
Raincoast Books
112 East Third Avenue
Vancouver, B.C.
V5T 1C8
10 9 8 7 6 5 4 3 2 1

Chronicle Books
San Francisco, California

ACKNOWLEDGEMENTS

Anne-Mette Abildgaard

David Barich

Cafe Trio, San Francisco

The staff at Cal-Mart, San Francisco

Debra Casserly

Ron Collier, Porter's Produce and Epicurean Giftbaskets, San Francisco

Charlotte Davis

Susan deVaty

Ruth Falk

Dexter Fedor

Stephanie Greenleigh

Kenneth Gwin

Jacqueline Jones

Joyce Jue

Bob Lambert

Bill LeBlond

Randy Lee, Petrini's Market, Stonestown, San Francisco

Jo Mancuso

Melissa McCumiskey

Linda McKenzie

Carlo Middione, Vivande Porta Via, San Francisco

Jennifer Morla

Lisa Osta

Phillip Quattrociocchi, San Francisco International Cheese Imports, San Francisco

Real Food Company, San Francisco, specifically Bert Brown, Jimmy Ilson, and Patrick LoCicero

Lois Reimer

Michael Schwab

Sara Slavin

Rod Smith and Dana DeKalb

William Stewart

Elizabeth Strohecker, California Sunshine Fine Foods, Inc., San Francisco

Mark Steisel

Peg Vasilak

Mary and Vicki VanDamme

Michael Watchorn and Warren Percell, The Hog Island Oyster Company, Marshall, California

Wendy White

I thought that if I ate the food of the area
that I was visiting,
That I might assimilate the point of view of
the people there.

...When shopping at the supermarket,
I felt a great desire to walk off with someone
else's groceries...

As though if I ate their groceries
I would become that person
until I finished the groceries
...Living identical lives as long as the groceries
lasted.

—David Byrne

*g*razing. That is what this book really is about. Many people dislike the term and the trendiness it represents, but I think it's accurate. □ A few years ago I found myself ordering several appetizers and foregoing the entree at restaurants. I liked the smaller portions, and that part of the menu seemed to be where the chefs concentrated their exciting flavor combinations and experiments. I was relieved when I heard grazing was a recognized phenomenon; my way of eating was accepted, and I no longer had to worry about offending restaurant staffs. □ So in a way, *Openers* is a misnomer. While restaurants would classify these dishes as "first courses," my intention is to have people mix and match them to create lighter meals, as is done with *tapas*. Certainly these recipes can be used for appetizers. But one can also dine lightly on one or two of these dishes, or entertain with a selection of several. We are no longer limited by the traditional concept of what constitutes a proper dinner. It follows that you will find a variety of dishes here—some elegant, others homey and extremely simple. □ My purpose has always been to provide food that nourishes the body, intrigues the palate, and pleases the eye. In 1986, I was privileged to enjoy a great dinner prepared by Philippe de Givenchy, a talented young chef whose philosophy, preparation, and presentation of food are much like my own. Some of the ideas that emerged from the discussion that evening are close to my own thinking: □ Today's food is really *cuisine personelle*, a personal cuisine that is an expression of the chef's or cook's vision. □ Simplicity: Less of what enhances—and sometimes disguises—and more of the choice ingredients themselves. What is the essential flavor of a dish, and how do you combine it with other flavors while retaining an integrity of taste? This "back to basics" approach stresses high-quality ingredients and encourages small producers of fine regional foods—a renaissance to be supported. □ The emergence of the *cuisine de la future*. Food is an exchange between cultures and friends; restaurants and patrons; generations; even cab drivers and their fares. Historically, the development of a culture's cuisine was slow, involving recipes handed down from one generation to another. Now this exchange happens extremely fast, largely through restaurants and the media. Food can be stylish and ephemeral. Some dishes will look dated in twenty years; others will endure. Out of this rapid cross-pollination, what will emerge as the new basics? □ A complicated mystique surrounds food. We appreciate it with our senses and our intellects. We find it in music, rituals, cultural events and historical accounts. □ There is also a mystique about cooking. People love to sit at *sushi* bars and watch the chef's wizardry. Even after an eleven-hour day of preparing food on a photo shoot, my legs aching from standing, I find myself on a Friday night at the counter of an *au courant* diner, watching the line chefs as the other patrons marvel at their efficiency and grace. We all love watching the spectacle of food being created. □ Cooking is a personal expression that draws on reserves of concentration and a never-ending desire to learn more. The cook can focus, draw inward, and create something that provides energy, pleasure, beauty, and a nourishing exchange with other people. □ I see *Openers* as a guideline for combining flavors. You could re-create the plates you see here, but better to see what shape of melon falls off your knife and let that inspire you. Don't fret if you have a naive beginner's hand or if the avocados seem too slippery; mastery will come. □ Since my business is food styling, I am constantly working with food. Usually my assignments are to "plate" and design settings for other people's recipes and products. I get to see, read, and prepare many recipes, and taste the results. Yet when it comes to fixing food for myself or others, I am usually in a hurry. Hence my recipes tend to be quite simple and last-minute, or the do-ahead-at-your-leisure type. My inspirations come from many sources: nature, travel, architecture, restaurants, friends — certainly all the people I ever cook and dine with. □ *Openers* is designed to be an opening into another level of awareness of food. It is a journal, a diary of memorable meals — a scrapbook of my own favorites. □ The ingredient still lifes in this book are moments preserved, intended to show off the specialness of foods that are transformed as the dishes are prepared. Trust your own intuition and experience, and use this book as a guide to deepen your view of appreciating and enjoying food.

— Amy Nathan

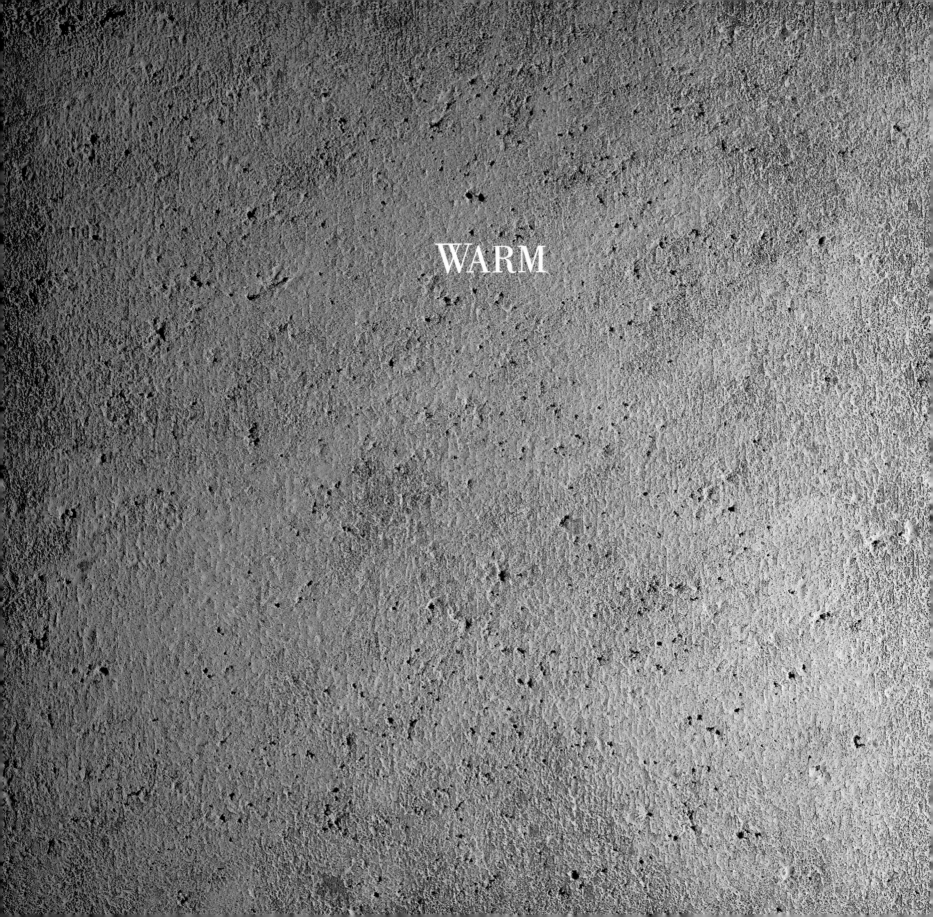

WARM

When the last goblins race away down your steps on All Hallows' Eve, pumpkins turn back into pumpkins. With Thanksgiving just a page away on the calendar, even a grinning jack-o-lantern starts to look like a vegetable again. This light, refreshing soup, which avoids the expected spices, can be made with pumpkin or acorn squash.

*P*lace pumpkins cut side down in a baking pan. Add water to a depth of 1 inch. Bake in a preheated 350° oven for 30 minutes. Let cool. Scrape pumpkin flesh from shell. You should have about 6 cups cooked pumpkin. □ Lay pumpkin seeds in a single layer on a baking sheet and sprinkle lightly with salt. Bake at 300° until lightly browned, stirring seeds a couple of times to prevent sticking. Reserve for garnish. □ In a large skillet or sauté pan, heat butter and oil. Sauté leeks for about 5 minutes, or until softened. Stir in 1 cup chicken broth. Lower heat and cover. Cook an additional 20 minutes. Set aside. In a stockpot, heat remaining chicken broth over medium heat. □ In a blender or food processor, puree pumpkin flesh in small batches, adding warmed chicken broth as necessary to liquefy. □ Add all pumpkin puree and chicken broth to stockpot. Add both the wines to stockpot, then salt and pepper to taste. Simmer partially covered for 30 minutes. □ Combine lime juice and sour cream in a small bowl. □ Serve soup with lime cream drizzled over it. Garnish with lime zest and a few pumpkin seeds. Pass additional lime cream and seeds. □ Serves 4.

2 medium pumpkins, halved, strings removed, and seeds reserved

Salt

4 tablespoons unsalted butter

2 tablespoons olive oil

2 bunches leeks, trimmed, washed well, and sliced thin

3 quarts chicken broth

½ cup dry white wine

⅓ cup Pineau de Charentes wine

Dash salt

White pepper

Zest and juice of 3 limes

1 cup sour cream

*P*repare pasta per package directions. □ In a large sauté pan or skillet, heat olive oil and sauté garlic for about 3 minutes. Add snap peas and sauté an additional 5 minutes, or until garlic just begins to brown. □ Serve a portion of each mixture side by side on individual plates. □ Serves 4.

⅓ pound melon-seed pasta or orzo

3 tablespoons olive oil

6 garlic cloves, coarsely chopped

1 pound sugar-snap peas, trimmed and cut lengthwise

Here is a study in contrasts: sweet and pungent, smooth and crunchy, vivid and neutral. But once you start eating this dish, you may not want to stop to ponder; your senses will have to work cooperatively. The peas still nestled in their halved pods are fun to see. The melon-seed pasta, also called orzo, is smooth and sweet, made with semolina. The peas and garlic chips are crunchy; the combination is sweet but has bite. This easy, last-minute dish is best enjoyed in late spring or late fall-early winter, when sugar snaps are in their prime.

Glistening in their narrow black shells, succulent mussels offer not only their own unique taste, but the flavors they readily absorb from whatever you spoon over them. The inexpensive shell-fish have accommodated themselves to cultivation: some mussel-ranchers even grow them on strings.

*d*ry-roast the mussels to open, as follows: Place mussels in a single layer in an all-metal skillet or sauté pan. Cover. Place over very high heat for 30 to 45 seconds. Check and remove mussels that are open. Repeat process, checking at 15-second intervals and removing mussels as they open. Run opened mussels under cool water. Drain and remove top shell. If desired, loosen each mussel from its shell. Return mussels to pan in a single layer. □ In a saucepan, melt butter. Add garlic, shallot, parsley, and walnuts. □ Drizzle some butter mixture over each mussel. □ Bake in a preheated 500° oven for about 5 minutes, or just until mussels are heated through. Serve hot. If desired, serve with parsleyed "soldier boys": Spread one long side of toast bars with soft butter and dip in minced parsley. □ Serves 4.

28 to 36 mussels, scrubbed and debearded

¾ cup (1½ sticks) unsalted butter

4 garlic cloves, finely chopped

1 shallot, minced

3 tablespoons chopped parsley

½ cup walnuts, toasted lightly and finely chopped

Lemon wedges (optional)

S almon Fillets Broiled with Lemons: Preheat broiler. □ Line a broiling pan with lemon slices. Place fillets over slices. Dot with butter and drizzle with fresh lemon juice. Place one or two lemon slices on each fillet. □ Broil 1 inch from heat for about 12 minutes, or until desired doneness. Cooking time will vary with thickness of fish. Thin areas of fillets can be protected from overcooking by covering with lemon slices if needed. □ On each of 4 individual serving plates, arrange 1 fillet plus some of the browned lemon "chips." Do not serve slices that supported fillets. □ Accompany with your choice of either mustard mayonnaise or lemon-mustard butter, and a dill sprig. □ Serves 4.

Mustard Mayonnaise: In a blender or food processor, combine egg, lemon juice, and mustard and process well. □ While machine is running, add olive oil slowly in a thin stream until incorporated. □ Makes 1 cup.

Lemon-Mustard Butter: Cream all ingredients together and let stand 1 hour in a cool place. □ Makes ½ cup.

SALMON FILLETS:

4 salmon fillets, 4 to 5 ounces each and as thick as possible

2 lemons, scrubbed and thinly sliced

Unsalted butter

Juice from 1 additional lemon

Dill sprigs for garnish

MUSTARD MAYONNAISE:

1 egg

1 tablespoon fresh lemon juice

1 tablespoon Dijon mustard

¾ cup light French olive oil

LEMON-MUSTARD BUTTER:

½ cup (1 stick) unsalted butter

½ teaspoon grated lemon zest

Juice of ½ lemon (preferably Meyer or another soft, ripe lemon)

2 tablespoons Dijon mustard

Dash freshly ground white pepper

Sweet, aromatic Meyer lemons are ideal in this dish. The fish is broiled between two layers of lemon slices—the bed keeps it from sticking, and the blanket keeps it moist and then turns into browned and crispy "lemon chips."

Monochromatic in its pale perfection, this version of a classic dish is creamy-simple and elegant. Risotto is a method of preparing rice by vigorous simmering and constant stirring, so that it absorbs flavorful liquids gradually. Dry champagne deepens and complicates the flavor, imparting a rich, yeasty quality.

*i*n a heavy saucepan over low heat, melt 2 table-spoons butter. Add olive oil and heat. Sauté onion until just soft. Do not brown. □ Add rice and sauté until well coated with oil. Add ½ cup broth and stir continually until it is almost absorbed. Repeat until all broth is incorporated. □ Begin adding champagne in ½-cup increments, stirring continually with each addition until liquid is almost all absorbed. Continue cooking and stirring until rice is *al dente*. Total cooking time will be about 30 minutes. □ Add remaining 1 tablespoon butter and Parmesan. Mix well. Serve immediately. □ Serves 6.

3 tablespoons unsalted butter

2 tablespoons olive oil

3 tablespoons minced white onion

1½ cups Arborio rice

2½ cups chicken broth, warmed

2½ cups dry champagne

½ cup grated imported Parmesan cheese

*C*ombine olive oil and vinegar; set aside. □ Heat a grill pan or ridged skillet on stovetop. Brush with oil. Place chicories cut side down and cook 1 to 2 minutes, or until they just begin to soften. Do not turn. Do *frisée* last as it cooks fastest. □ Arrange one of each kind of chicory on individual plates, cut side up. Drizzle with vinaigrette and sprinkle with pistachios. Serve. □ *Notes:* To grill over charcoal: Brush chicories with vinaigrette. Let stand 15 minutes. Drain. Over low-glowing coals, grill very briefly or until lightly seared. □ Serves 4.

½ cup extra-virgin Italian olive oil

6 tablespoons sherry wine vinegar

Olive oil for grill pan

2 heads radicchio, halved

2 heads Belgian endive, halved

2 heads frisée, halved

¼ cup unsalted pistachios, chopped

Once-exotic European chicories seem to rule the salad plate these days. Succulent Belgian endive; curly, slightly bitter frisée; and the even sharper red radicchio are usually mixed with more familiar greens, but here they stand distinctively on their own. Grilling—either on the stovetop in a grill pan, or on the barbecue—renders their flavors milder, while a light coat of dressing is absorbed into the leaves.

A little stovetop alchemy turns onions into marmalade: they are first tamed by simmering in vinegar, then take on the quality of preserves as they cook in honey. A simple white-fleshed fish such as halibut or sea bass makes the perfect partner for this aromatic and pungent sauce—a bit sweet, a bit sour.

*C*ut fish fillets in half; place them in a baking pan and rub them with 3 tablespoons olive oil. Press buttered parchment on surfaces of fish and bake in a preheated 375° oven for about 20 minutes, or until fish just begins to flake. □ In a large sauté pan or skillet, heat ¼ cup olive oil and sauté onion until translucent, about 7 minutes. □ Stir in vinegar, honey, and paprika. Cook over medium heat, stirring occasionally, another 7 minutes, or until liquid is reduced and onions are caramelized. Pool some sauce on individual serving plates. Place fish on sauce. Garnish with fresh chervil. Serve hot. □ Serves 4.

2 thick white fish fillets, such as halibut, turbot, or orange roughy (about ½ pound each)

3 tablespoons olive oil

Parchment for baking

¼ cup olive oil

2 large onions, sliced thin

½ cup red wine vinegar

⅓ cup honey

½ teaspoon paprika

Fresh chervil for garnish

*i*n a large saucepan, whisk together chicken broth and coconut milk. □ Add chicken, green onions, yellow onion, and ginger and heat to just below boiling. Lower heat and simmer 15 to 20 minutes, until chicken is opaque and tender. □ Add lemon grass, pepper flakes, cilantro, mushrooms, and zest. Cook another 5 minutes. □ Add milk and cook another 10 minutes, until heated through. Stir in fish sauce, garnish with cilantro, and serve. □ Serves 6.

One 14-ounce can chicken broth

One 14-ounce can coconut milk

2 chicken breast halves and 2 thighs, skinned, boned, and cut into strips

3 green onions, sliced

½ medium yellow onion, chopped

3 diagonal slices fresh ginger

2 stalks lemon grass, sliced, or ½ teaspoon powdered dried lemon grass or dried lemon peel

½ teaspoon dried red pepper flakes

2 tablespoons coarsely chopped cilantro

One 10- to 15-ounce can straw mushrooms, drained

Zest of 1 lemon

1½ cups milk

3 tablespoons fish sauce (nam pla)

Cilantro sprigs for garnish

This recipe demystifies the classic dish tom ka gai, preserving the spirit and flavor of that aromatic soup in an uncomplicated, accessible way. Even those unfamiliar with the Thai palate often are captivated at the first taste.

The earthly pleasures of mushrooms are right at our feet—or in the bins of the specialty greengrocer. Rich-tasting exotic varieties—sensually textured umbrella-capped shiitakes; fragile-tasting clumps of deeply gilled oyster mushrooms; mild, meaty chanterelles shaped like furled trumpet flowers— are mixed here with ordinary white buttons in a dish that could foreshadow a beef or veal entree.

*i*f time allows, soak rice in very warm water for several hours, until grains begin to split. In a very large sauté pan or skillet, heat 2 tablespoons butter and sauté shallots and carrots for 2 minutes. Add white mushrooms and sauté until tender. Deglaze pan with ¾ cup chicken broth and reduce heat to low. Cover. Simmer for 5 minutes. In a covered stockpot, warm remaining chicken broth. □ In a blender or food processor, puree mushroom mixture by adding 1½ cups of warmed broth in ½-cup increments. Return pureed mixture to stockpot and continue heating. □ In a sauté pan or skillet, heat remaining 3 tablespoons butter and sauté exotic mushrooms until they just begin to brown. Deglaze pan with cognac. Add to stockpot. □ Add rice, chopped herbs, salt, and pepper. Simmer covered until rice is fully cooked. Serve with a sprinkling of chopped chives. □ *Notes:* Cooking the rice in the soup will add flavor, but adding cooked rice works and does save time. Remember that dried herbs intensify with cooking time, while fresh herbs weaken. □ Serves 6 to 8.

1 cup wild rice

6 shallots, sliced thin

1 carrot, rough chopped

5 tablespoons unsalted butter

½ pound white mushrooms, sliced

2½ quarts unsalted chicken broth

¾ to 1 pound mixed exotic mushrooms, such as shiitake, oyster, and chanterelle (slice if large, leave whole if small)

¼ cup cognac, Calvados, or brandy for deglazing

2 to 3 teaspoons chopped fresh thyme

1 teaspoon chopped fresh savory

1 tablespoon chopped parsley

White pepper and salt to taste

Chives for garnish

*b*lanch or steam asparagus until tender. Cut into 1-inch pieces. Divide stalk segments between 4 small ramekins. Set tips aside. □ Beat together eggs, cream, and nutmeg. □ Melt butter in a nonstick skillet and gently scramble eggs until barely set. □ Divide among ramekins. Top each ramekin with asparagus tips and a sprinkling of nutmeg. Serve immediately. □ Serves 4.

4 stalks asparagus
bases, peeled if desired

8 fresh large eggs

¼ cup heavy cream

⅛ teaspoon
freshly grated nutmeg

1 tablespoon unsalted butter

Nutmeg for sprinkling

The mild-mannered egg, so versatile and compatible with other foods, is a natural for first courses like souffles and quiches. Here the egg is 'un-disguised,' prepared simply and served elegantly. If you are fortunate enough to find it, try the prized white asparagus, lacking the usual color because it has been covered with soil before the spears are exposed to light.

Few sensations can comfort like the familiar crunch and melt of a perfect grilled-cheese sandwich. This simple update shows how ingredients chosen for flavor and quality—not complicated preparation—can make a dish special and satisfying.

*M*elt 2 tablespoons butter in a sauté pan and sauté mushrooms until tender. □ Lay out 4 slices of bread. Top each with a slice of cheese and some mushrooms. Sprinkle with herbs. Top each with another cheese slice and other slice of bread. Press together. □ Lightly pan-fry sandwiches in a little butter, turning once. □ Cut each sandwich into 3 bars and top each with an herb sprig. Serve hot. □ Serves 4.

2 tablespoons unsalted butter

½ pound white mushrooms, sliced thin

8 thin slices whole-wheat bread, crusts removed

8 thin slices mozzarella cheese

Chopped fresh oregano or marjoram

Butter for frying

Herb sprigs for garnish

*g*reen Tomatoes and Lamb: Rub lamb tenderloin with 2 tablespoons olive oil, garlic clove, and rosemary branch. Bake in a preheated 400° oven for about 20 minutes, or until an instant-read thermometer registers 130° (for medium rare). Remove from oven and leave oven at 400° for garlic. Allow to cool before slicing. □ Prepare garlic puree; set aside. □ Heat olive oil for frying in a sauté pan or skillet and sauté tomato slices, turning once, until they just begin to soften. □ Arrange individual plates with tomato slices, lamb slices, and garlic puree. Garnish with whole roasted garlic cloves and a sprig of rosemary. □ Serves 4.

Garlic Puree: Cut off tops of garlic heads. Place heads in a shallow pan with 1 inch of water. Roast at 400° for 30 minutes, or until soft. Let cool. Reserve 1 head garlic for garnish. Squeeze remaining garlic from heads directly into a blender or food processor. Add potato and ½ teaspoon olive oil and puree to the consistency of a smooth paste.

GREEN TOMATOES AND LAMB:

1 lamb tenderloin (about 1¼ pounds)

2 tablespoons olive oil

1 garlic clove, halved

1 rosemary branch

2 green tomatoes, thickly sliced

Olive oil for frying

Rosemary sprigs for garnish

GARLIC PUREE:

3 garlic heads

1 small white potato, peeled and boiled

½ teaspoon olive oil

Plucking a few garden tomatoes when they are still green won't defuse late summer's explosion of ripe fruit, and you can enjoy a few while they are still tart and firm. The lamb tenderloin can be roasted ahead and served at room temperature, although it is good hot, too. The ubiquitous garlic, found today in everything from salad to ice cream, here resumes its customary place alongside lamb. After the entire bulb is roasted, the contents slide easily from their clove jackets and are pureed with a little potato to soften the flavor.

Cultivated since the days of the early Romans for its fleshy root, the sweet, delicate, and slightly nut-ty-flavored parsnip is often passed over today in favor of its close relative, the carrot. Here the proletarian parsnip teams up with the rarefied spice saffron—made from the dried orange-red stig-mas of crocus flowers—in a fancy, do-ahead timbale.

*P*arsnip Timbales: Pare and slice parsnips. Cook in boiling water to cover until easily pierced with a fork, about 5 minutes. Drain and pat dry. In a blender or food processor, puree parsnips and eggs. Remove to a bowl. Whisk in cream, salt, and pepper. Pour into 4 lightly buttered ¾-cup ramekins. □ Place ramekins in a baking pan and add hot water to reach halfway up sides. Bake in a preheated 325° oven for approximately 35 to 40 minutes, or until centers are set. If using smaller ramekins, decrease baking time to 30 minutes. Remove and let cool for 10 minutes. Run a knife around timbales and unmold them onto waxed paper. Keep warm. □ Prepare sauce. □ To serve, pool some sauce onto each of 4 serving plates. Place a timbale in center of sauce. Surround with some of each type of seafood. Place a few saffron threads in sauce. Garnish each timbale with chives and blossoms. Serve warm. □ Serves 4.

Sauce: Melt butter in a heavy saucepan. Stir in flour and cook 2 minutes over low heat. Add wine and stock and continue cooking and stirring for 3 minutes. Add saffron cream, bring to a boil, and cook until reduced by half, about 10 minutes.

TIMBALES:

*3 large parsnips
(to equal 1 cup cooked)*

3 eggs

1 cup heavy cream

¼ teaspoon salt

*⅛ teaspoon
ground white pepper*

Butter for ramekins

SAUCE:

2 tablespoons unsalted butter

1 tablespoon flour

¼ cup fruity white wine

1 cup fish stock

*Generous ¼ teaspoon
saffron threads soaked in
½ cup heavy cream*

SEAFOOD:

1 large lobster tail, boiled

*24 mussels, scrubbed,
debearded, and steamed*

*One ½- to 1-pound white fish
such as halibut, monkfish,
or haddock, poached*

GARNISH:

*Additional saffron threads,
snipped chives,
and chive blossoms*

*W*ild Rice Pancakes: In a large bowl, combine dry ingredients. Add rice. Beat milk and egg yolks together well, then add to rice mixture. Beat egg whites until stiff but not dry. Fold egg whites into batter. On a hot, greased griddle, pour batter to make 4-inch pancakes. Keep warm. □ Prepare sauce. □ Allow 3 pancakes per person. Top each serving with some of the shredded duck and sauce. Serve hot. □ Serves 4.

Sauce: In a saucepan, heat apricot nectar and wine until boiling. Let boil for 15 minutes to reduce. Combine cornstarch with *tamari* and lemon juice and whisk into sauce. Whisk and reduce until clarified and thickened, about 5 minutes.

PANCAKES:

2 cups whole-wheat
pastry flour

3 teaspoons baking powder

1 teaspoon salt

2 cups cooked wild rice

2 cups milk soured with
2 tablespoons lemon juice

2 eggs, separated

SAUCE:

2 cups apricot nectar

1 cup Gewürztraminer wine

1 tablespoon cornstarch

1 tablespoon tamari

1 tablespoon lemon juice

MEAT:

Meat from 1 cooked duck,
shredded and set aside

Whether harvested by the Chippewa Indians from Northern Minnesota's lakes or paddy-grown in California's fertile Lake County, wild rice is a delicate, nutty grain joined here with another food steeped in cultural tradition: crispy-skinned roast duck, found hanging in the deli windows of almost any Chinatown. If roast duck is not available, smoked chicken or broiled duck breasts may be substituted.

COOL

San Francisco chef Daniel Malzhan is responsible for the unusual flavor combination in this soup. The smooth, mild cantaloupe makes a perfect base on which to float contrasting sensations. Wasabi cream injects a hot zest, and ginger adds bite. This makes a quick, refreshing dish in warm weather.

*C*antaloupe Soup: In a blender or food processor, puree cantaloupe. □ Add grape juice, buttermilk, and lime juice and process again. □ To obtain a smoother consistency, remove mixture from machine and re-process in two smaller batches. □ Chill or serve at room temperature. □ Garnish individual bowls with a swirl of *wasabi* cream, some julienned fresh ginger, and a borage blossom. □ Makes 3½ cups, serves about 4.

Wasabi Cream: Combine *wasabi* powder and water. Let stand 5 minutes. □ Combine yogurt and milk. Blend until smooth. □ Combine *wasabi* and yogurt mixtures.

CANTALOUPE SOUP:

1 very ripe cantaloupe, seeded and peeled

½ cup white grape juice (Riesling, if available)

¾ cup low-fat buttermilk

1 tablespoon fresh lime juice

½-inch piece fresh ginger, peeled and cut into fine julienne

Borage blossoms for garnish

WASABI CREAM:

¾ teaspoon wasabi powder (available in Japanese markets)

1 tablespoon water

2 tablespoons yogurt

2 to 3 tablespoons milk

*b*asil Variations: In a sauté pan or skillet, bring 2 inches of water to a very gentle boil. Add vinegar and salt. Poach eggs in liquid. As yolks begin to set (about 5 minutes), transfer eggs with a slotted spatula to a shallow pan of cool water to hold for serving. □ Blanch or steam beans for approximately 5 minutes, or until tender. Rinse under cold water, drain, and cut lengthwise. Set aside. □ Cut half of basil leaves into thin strips. Set them aside, reserving whole leaves for garnish. In a large bowl, combine olive oil and sherry vinegar. Toss beans in mixture to coat. □ Divide beans among 4 serving plates. Sprinkle each serving with basil strips and bacon. Top each with one poached egg. (Be sure to allow excess water to run off eggs before placing over beans). □ Sprinkle with cracked pepper and add some whole basil leaves to each plate. □ Serve with baguette toasts topped with *pesto* spread. □ Serves 4.

Pesto Spread: In a blender or food processor, puree garlic and pine nuts. □ Add basil, parsley, butter, and oil. Process until mixture becomes a thick paste. □ Remove to a bowl. Fold in Parmesan cheese. □ Makes 1 cup.

BASIL VARIATIONS:

4 small fresh eggs

2 tablespoons vinegar for poaching

1 tablespoon salt

1 pound yellow wax beans, ends trimmed

1 handful each green and opal basil leaves, mixed

¼ cup olive oil

3 tablespoons sherry wine vinegar

3 bacon slices, cooked and crumbled

Cracked black pepper

8 thin baguette slices, toasted lightly

PESTO SPREAD:

4 large garlic cloves

2 tablespoons pine nuts

1 cup basil leaves, firmly packed

⅓ cup flat-leaf parsley leaves, firmly packed

2 tablespoons unsalted butter, softened

3 tablespoons olive oil

½ cup grated Parmesan cheese

Where "food" is spoken, basil often translates simply as pesto, an exquisite, almost irresistible way to enjoy this favorite herb. Yet the silky, creased leaves have a delightful versatility; look for many varieties of basil, like opal, lemon, cinnamon, or Thai. Here a small poached egg acts as a wonderful, unexpected dressing atop waxed beans.

There's more than a kernel of truth to the notion of corn as a dietary mainstay—sliced and boiled, steamed, roasted or pulverized into mush, it has fed hungry hordes down through the centuries. From lightly dressed "seeds" to a delicate custard to sturdy polenta triangles— even the papery husk takes its place in this virtuoso dish, which demonstrates the versatility of a sometimes overlooked staple. Each corn plate consists of a serving of corn and shrimp salad, corn custard, and a polenta triangle. All three may be made ahead, leaving only the cheese melting and plate assembly for serving time. A good instant polenta mix will save on preparation time.

*C*orn and Bay Shrimp Salad: Steam corn 8 to 10 minutes. Rinse under cold water. Drain and pat dry with paper towels. □ In a large bowl, combine corn, shrimp, and parsley. □ In a small bowl, whisk together vinegar, oil, and pepper flakes. Pour over corn mixture and stir to coat entire mixture. □ Serve immediately, or chill to meld flavors. □ Serves 4.

Corn Custard: In a large bowl, whisk together eggs, milk, and cream. □ Stir in Tabasco, corn, and cheese. □ Ladle into four buttered ½-cup ramekins. □ Set ramekins in a baking dish. Add hot water to reach halfway up sides of ramekins. Bake in a preheated 350° oven for 30 minutes, or until a knife inserted in center of each custard comes out clean. □ Remove from baking dish and allow custards to cool. If you wish to unmold custards, let them cool thoroughly, run a sharp knife around edges, and invert on waxed paper. Tap bottom of ramekins. Invert again to serve. Top with red pepper strips. Serve at room temperature. □ Serves 4.

Polenta Triangles: In a large saucepan, bring water to a boil. Add salt. □ Add polenta very slowly, stirring continually with a wooden spoon. □ Reduce heat to low and simmer, stirring, until polenta is thick and smooth. □ Pour into a lightly greased 8-inch-square pan. Let cool until firm. □ Cut polenta into triangles and top each with a smaller triangle of cheese. □ Just before serving, heat polenta triangles for a few minutes in a preheated 300° oven or in a skillet over low heat until cheese softens. □ Serves 4.

CORN AND BAY SHRIMP SALAD:

10 ounces corn kernels

1 cup bay shrimp

½ cup coarsely chopped parsley

2 tablespoons champagne vinegar

¼ cup light olive oil

¼ teaspoon dried red pepper flakes

CORN CUSTARD:

3 eggs, beaten

¾ cup milk

½ cup heavy cream

3 drops Tabasco sauce

1 cup corn kernels, steamed

¼ cup grated Monterey jack cheese

Butter for ramekins

Red bell pepper strips for garnish

POLENTA TRIANGLES:

5 cups water

1 teaspoon salt

1½ cups polenta corn meal

2 slices Monterey jack cheese

*S*tuffing: Heat butter in a sauté pan or skillet. Sauté shallots in butter until they are translucent. Add currants and pine nuts and cook, stirring, until nuts are golden. Combine with rice. Set aside.

Meat: In a large non-stick skillet over medium-high heat, sear outside of pork loin. Transfer to a board. □ Unroll pork loin into a single piece. Lay enough spinach leaves over meat to cover surface. □ Spread rice mixture gently down center of pork loin, leaving a 1½-inch margin along all sides. □ Beginning at one end, roll meat like a jelly roll and tie with cotton string at 2-inch intervals. □ Roast in a preheated 400° oven for 60 minutes. □ Let cool to room temperature. Slice and serve with Apricot-*Jalapeño* Sauce. □ Serves 8.

Apricot-*Jalapeño* Sauce: In a saucepan, combine dried apricots, canned apricots, and bourbon. Bring to a boil, then reduce to lowest heat and simmer uncovered 30 minutes. □ Remove from heat, cover, and cool. □ Transfer mixture to a food processor and pulse 6 times, or puree coarsely in a blender. □ Remove to a bowl and stir in *jalapeños*, cumin, red pepper, lime juice, and zest. □ Makes 2 cups.

STUFFING:

2 tablespoons unsalted butter

2 shallots, chopped

¼ cup currants

¼ cup pine nuts

1 cup cooked basmati rice

MEAT:

1 pork tenderloin (1 to 1¼ pounds), butterflied and rubbed with fresh garlic

½ pound spinach, cleaned and stems removed

APRICOT-JALAPEÑO SAUCE:

4 ounces dried apricots, diced

One 16-ounce can apricots, halves drained

¾ cup bourbon whiskey

4 jalapeño peppers, seeded and very finely diced

½ teaspoon ground cumin

¼ teaspoon dried red pepper flakes

Zest and juice of 1 lime

The combination of pork and fruit
is a classic one, yet with its spin-
ach-wrapped rice, the center of this
pork roll is more like a version of sushi.
An impressive-looking dish, it can be prepared in advance and served at room temperature.

Unlike other meats that are assertive in company, veal is somewhat retiring and will show off an unlikely pairing of sweet raspberry and salty tomato. Pear-shaped Romas—supple _pumate_ are the best—are neater and more flavorful than their rounded cousins when sun-dried and cured in olive oil.

Veal with Sun-Dried Tomatoes and Raspberry Vinaigrette

*r*ub veal roast with 2 tablespoons olive oil. □ Roast in a preheated 400° oven for 25 minutes. □ Let cool to room temperature. Chill, if desired. □ Slice veal as thin as possible and arrange slices on individual serving plates. Sprinkle tomato strips over meat. □ Whisk together olive oil and raspberry vinegar. Drizzle over veal. □ Add a sprig of watercress to each plate. □ Serves 6.

1 pound veal loin roast

2 tablespoons olive oil

6 sun-dried tomatoes, drained and cut into strips

½ cup light olive oil

6 tablespoons raspberry vinegar

Watercress for garnish

SARDINE PLATE

*O*pen sardines carefully and drain off excess oil. □ Break crackers into a size appropriate to sardines. Top with a sardine or two and a slice of lemon. □ Place 3 cracker canapes on each individual serving plate along with some cucumber, sorrel, and tomatoes. □ Serves 4.

1 tin good-quality sardines

Rye crackers or crispbread

*1 lemon, scrubbed
and very thinly sliced*

*1 pickling cucumber,
very thinly sliced*

*1 bunch sorrel,
cut into ¾-inch strips*

*Handful yellow pear tomatoes,
halved lengthwise*

Long consigned to the unglamorous
lunchbox, the often overlooked sardine is more
than nutrition in a tin. Good-quality sardines, caught in
waters off the coasts of France, Portugal, and Spain, are
gently brined, properly dried, lightly cooked in olive oil, and
stored for a year so that fish and oil flavors may mingle.

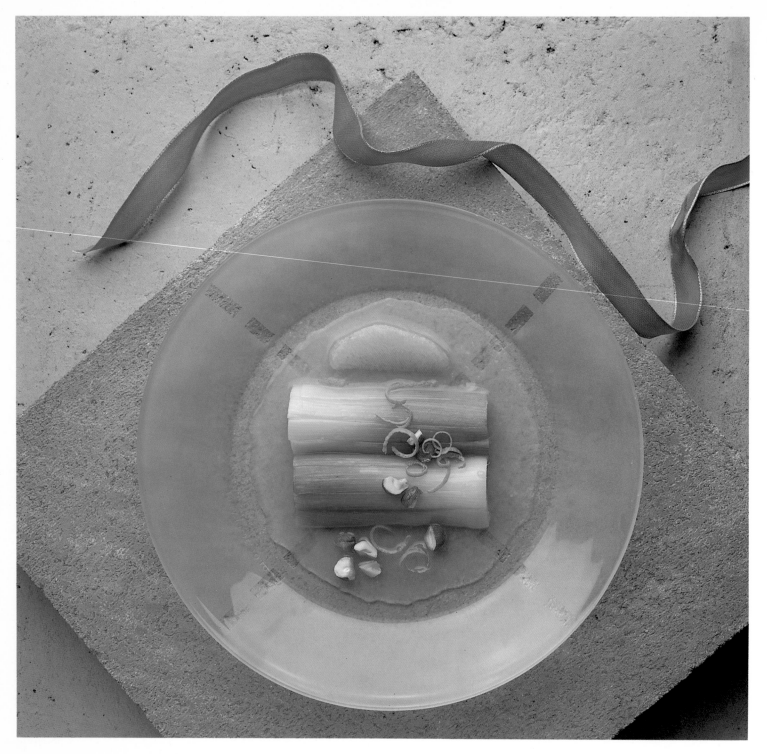

The tender leek is a mild-flavored member of the onion clan, a grown-up cousin of the scallion. Here clean-tasting leeks are arranged on the plate in a way that emphasizes their delicate white-to-green gradation.

*C*ut leeks into 4-inch segments to include color gradation from white to pale green. Split leeks lengthwise and place them in a flat-bottomed steamer over boiling water. □ Steam 10 to 15 minutes, or until leeks are tender but not mushy. Remove steamer from heat. Run cold water over leeks to stop cooking process. Allow to cool. □ Using a spatula, carefully transfer leeks to a cutting surface. Using a very sharp knife, cut each leek lengthwise into 4 strips, being careful not to disturb its shape.□ Using a spatula, place 2 sliced leek halves on each serving plate, reversing 1 leek half so color gradation is opposite to other half.□ In a bowl, whisk together orange juice, Lillet, vinegar, and oil. Drizzle over leeks. □ Add orange segments, zest, and hazelnuts to plates in an arrangement that pleases you. □ Serves 4.

4 leeks, approximately
2 inches in diameter,
washed thoroughly

2 tablespoons
orange juice

2 tablespoons blonde Lillet

2 tablespoons
champagne vinegar

¼ cup hazelnut
or walnut oil

Zest and segments of 1 orange

3 tablespoons hazelnuts,
toasted and coarsely chopped

*a*vocado Crumble Salad: Arrange zucchini and avocado slices on individual serving plates as in photo. □ Spoon tomato *coulis* inside zucchini border. □ Sprinkle parsley and olives over avocados. □ Crumble corn bread over all. □ Serves 4.

Roma Tomato Coulis: Cut an X at the base of each tomato. Blanch tomatoes. Peel and seed them over a strainer, returning juice to tomato pulp. □ In a blender or food processor, puree pulp and juice. The mixture should not be totally smooth. □ Transfer mixture to a saucepan. Heat to boiling, reduce to a simmer, and cook for 5 minutes. □ Add herbs, white pepper, salt, and sherry and cook an additional 3 minutes. Let cool before serving. □ Makes 2 cups.

AVOCADO CRUMBLE SALAD:

2 zucchini,
sliced lengthwise, seeded,
and cut into very thin slices

1 to 2 avocados,
sliced and coated
with lemon or lime juice

¼ cup flat-leaf parsley,
coarsely chopped

16 niçoise olives

4 slices corn bread or muffins

ROMA TOMATO COULIS:

12 Roma (pear) tomatoes

¼ teaspoon
dried herbes de Provence

¼ teaspoon ground white pepper

⅛ teaspoon salt

1 tablespoon dry sherry

With its zucchini, tomato, and niçoise olives, this salad is steeped in the Mediterranean palate, and palette. But if you want to emphasize the taste of the American Southwest, substitute just one ingredient: cilantro for flat-leaf parsley. This dish gives new life to leftover corn bread, which dries out so quickly.

You can put the bite in — or take the bite out of — this traditional French snack through your choice of radishes. Gorgeous Flamboyants are mild and easy to digest, while sweet butter — Normandy, if you can find it, is best — will create a perfect foil for the more pungent 'redskins.'

Radish and Butter Sandwiches

Spread baguette bases with unsalted butter. □ Arrange radish fans over butter. □ Serve open-face, with small portions of salt, pepper, and chives. □ Serves 4.

1 baguette,
cut into 4 segments
and split lengthwise

½ cup (1 stick)
unsalted butter, softened

2 bunches radishes,
thinly sliced into fans

Coarse salt

Cracked black pepper

Chives,
snipped into ½-inch bars

*C*ut two-thirds of orange segments in half. Set aside. Reserve whole segments for garnish. In a saucepan, cook cranberries in 1 inch of water just until skins begin to pop. Drain cranberries and place them in a large bowl. Drizzle cranberries with honey to coat. □ Add rice, chicken, walnuts, and orange half-segments to cranberries. □ Whisk together juice of 1 orange, champagne vinegar, and walnut oil. Pour over rice mixture and toss to coat. □ Refrigerate salad 1 to 2 hours or overnight. □ Serve at room temperature with reserved whole orange segments for garnish. □ *Note:* This salad also works well with turkey or smoked chicken. Decrease chilling time if using smoked chicken, as its flavor will be too strong. □ Serves 6 to 8.

3 oranges, peeled and segmented

¼ pound cranberries

2 tablespoons honey

½ pound wild rice, cooked and cooled

2 boned and skinned chicken breast halves, poached and shredded

1¼ cups walnuts, toasted and chopped

Juice of 1 orange

2 tablespoons champagne vinegar

½ cup walnut oil

Toss wild rice and
cranberries left over
from Thanksgiving with
poached chicken for a satisfying salad of contrasting colors and
flavors. A walnut-oil dressing takes the
edge off the deliciously tart cranberries, and
the combination of fruits gives the salad a fresh
taste. Although it has a fall feeling, this dish is great
for summer, too.

Lime chili paste,
which has its roots
in the hotter palates
of Thai and Indonesian
cooking, resembles nothing
so much as a hot variation on
pesto. Shrimp chips start out as
discs, but explode into pastel curl-
icues when fried in hot oil.

*i*n a bowl, toss shrimp with salt. Let stand 1 hour. Rinse and pat dry with paper towels. □ In a large sauté pan or skillet, heat 2 to 3 tablespoons peanut oil and sauté shrimp quickly over high heat until they begin to char. Remove shrimp from heat. Drain. □ In a blender or food processor, puree chilies and juice of 3 limes. Add mint leaves and blend until mixture is completely pureed and consistency of a thick paste. You may need to add juice of an additional lime to obtain proper consistency. □ Fry shrimp chips in peanut oil as package directs. □ Serve shrimp with a dollop of the chili paste and a few sprigs of cilantro. Accompany with shrimp chips. □ Serves 4.

12 large shrimp, peeled and deveined

3 tablespoons salt

2 to 3 tablespoons peanut oil

3 jalapeño chilies, seeded and roughly chopped

Juice of 3 to 4 limes

1 cup mint leaves, firmly packed

Shrimp chips (available in Asian markets)

Peanut oil for frying

Cilantro sprigs

*C*ut honeydew into 4 wedges and enough chunks to make ¾ cup, then cut the remainder into tiny melon balls. □ In a blender or food processor, puree honeydew chunks and yogurt. Remove from container and stir in minced dill. □ To serve, pool yogurt sauce on individual plates. Top with some lettuce, trout, and melon balls. Place one melon wedge on each plate; garnish with additional dill sprigs. □ Serves 4.

2 honeydew melons, seeded

1 cup low-fat yogurt

2 tablespoons minced fresh dill

1 head limestone lettuce, cut into chiffonnade

1 large or 2 small smoked trout, skinned, boned, and flaked

Dill sprigs for garnish

Smoked fish makes an elegant starter course. Moist, soft fleshed trout is flaky and rich but light. Here its usual counterpart, cucumber, is replaced with honeydew melon. Used in this unaccustomed savory way, the melon is refreshing and cuts the high oil content of the fish.

As wild native stocks of traditionally harvested oysters on the East Coast are gradually depleted, the West Coast has spawned farms where oysters are cultured. From British Columbia to California, oysters are cultivated from "seedlings"; when they grow big enough, they are suspended in mesh bags in open bay waters to mature.

*O*yster Sampler: Allow 6 to 8 oysters per person. If you have your supplier open them, you can hold oysters refrigerated and on ice for a couple of hours. If you open them yourself, be sure to use a good-quality oyster knife and a heavy glove. □ If you wish, embellish larger oysters with a little lettuce and a lemon slice. □ Arrange an assortment of oysters and ginger chips on each plate. Serve immediately with the 2 *mignonette* sauces. □ Serves 4.

Ginger Chips: In a deep heavy pan, heat oil to 350° to 375°. □ Fry ginger slices in small batches until they begin to brown. Remove slices from oil with a slotted spoon and drain them well on paper towels. Reheat chips in a preheated 275° oven for a few minutes to crisp before serving. □ *Note:* It is best to fry these ahead, and reheat them just before serving to crisp.

Mignonette Sauce: Combine all ingredients. □ Makes ½ cup.

Tamari Mignonette Sauce: Combine all ingredients. □ Makes ½ cup.

OYSTER SAMPLER:

24 to 32 oysters of several varieties

3 limestone lettuce leaves, cut into chiffonnade

1 lemon, scrubbed, very thinly sliced, and cut into quarter rounds

GINGER CHIPS:

Oil for frying

One 4-inch piece of fresh ginger, peeled and thinly sliced

MIGNONETTE SAUCE:

¼ cup champagne vinegar

¼ cup dry white wine

1 teaspoon minced shallots

TAMARI MIGNONETTE SAUCE:

¼ cup rice vinegar

¼ cup mirin (available in Japanese markets)

1 tablespoon tamari sauce

1 teaspoon minced shallots

*i*n a large bowl, toss together bread, romaine, water-cress, and capers. □ Whisk together vinegar, oil, *fines herbes*, and horseradish. Pour over bread and lettuce mixture and toss well. □ To serve, arrange some beef strips on each plate. Add a portion of bread mixture. □ Serves 4.

2½ cups day-old herb bread, torn into cubes

1 head romaine lettuce, torn into 1-inch strips

1 bunch watercress, stemmed

¼ cup capers, drained

⅓ cup champagne vinegar

½ cup green Italian olive oil

¼ teaspoon fines herbes

1 tablespoon prepared horseradish

¾ pound New York strip steak, trimmed of excess fat, cooked rare, and cut into ¼-inch slices

In parts of Tuscany and Rome, stale bread soaked in water and then squeezed is added to a vegetable salad in proportion to the family's hunger. This hearty, peppery version is a "cut above," with its strips of broiled New York steak and solid chunks of rosemary bread tossed in horseradish vinaigrette.

FINGER FOOD

Learning
all the angles
for these cana-
pes is easy—the tri-
angles within squares
practically arrange them-
selves on plate or tray. Use
separate spreaders to keep black
edges black and white edges white.

*P*lace *chèvre* and *tapenade* in separate small bowls, each with a spreader. □ Visualize a diagonal dividing a biscuit in half. Carefully spread the lower right half with *tapenade* and the upper left half with *chèvre*. Repeat for all biscuits. Sprinkle with chives. □ Arrange canapes on an imaginary grid to form a checkerboard pattern. □ Serve soon after assembling, so that crackers will remain crisp. □ *Note:* The amounts of ingredients needed for this recipe will vary depending on the size of the biscuits and the number of canapes desired. The biscuits shown are from Jacob's Assorted Biscuits for cheese. Maniscottes (mini-toasts) also work well. □ Makes 24 pieces.

24 small biscuits, about 1¼ inches square

6 ounces mild chèvre

3 ounces tapenade, drained on paper towels

Snipped chives

(See note)

*b*eat 4 tablespoons (½ stick) butter in a sauté pan and sauté chicken strips 1 minute on each side. Remove chicken to a large bowl. Set aside. □ Add celery and onion to sauté pan and cook 10 minutes. Stir in parsley. Add this mixture to chicken. □ Combine cream and mustard in sauté pan and bring to a boil. Lower heat to medium and cook 1 minute. Reduce heat to low. Add cheese and simmer 8 minutes to reduce and thicken. Combine sauce and chicken vegetable mixture. Let cool. □ Blanch carrots and asparagus for 1 minute and cool immediately in ice water. Pat dry with paper towels. □ Melt remaining butter. □ Prepare to assemble strudels by laying down a thin damp cotton towel or a sheet of waxed paper. Unfold one sheet of *filo* over cloth, brush with melted butter, and sprinkle with bread crumb mixture. Top with another sheet of *filo* and repeat process for a total of 3 sheets. □ With the long side of *filo* toward you and working in the lower quarter of surface area, arrange filling ingredients as follows: Lay 2 asparagus and 2 carrot strips end to end. Place one-half of chicken mixture over strips, aligning chicken pieces with length of strudel. Place 2 more asparagus spears and carrot strips on either side and on top of chicken mixture. □ With help from the cloth below, lift edge closest to you and roll tightly to other end. Butter edge to seal. Tuck in ends. Repeat for second strudel. □ Bake in a preheated 325° oven for 20 minutes, or until golden. Cool before slicing. □ Makes 2 strudels, about 10 pieces each.

1 cup (2 sticks) unsalted butter

2 chicken breast halves, skinned, boned, and cut lengthwise into ¾-inch strips

1 cup chopped celery

1 onion, chopped

⅓ cup chopped parsley

1 cup heavy cream

⅓ cup Dijon mustard

3 ounces Gruyère cheese, grated

1 large carrot, peeled and sliced lengthwise into ⅛-inch julienne

8 thin asparagus spears, trimmed to 7-inch lengths

6 sheets filo *dough*

¾ cup coarse bread crumbs combined with ¾ cup coarsely ground toasted almonds

Slices of this savory hors d'oeuvre
reveal little cross-sections of its ingredients, which gastronomic geolo-
gists are invited to explore. Other din-
ers will probably be content simply to
enjoy the mosaic created by the
chicken and vegetables. Moist and
firm, much like a pâté, the strudel
is neither bready nor messy to eat.

In these light, savory tartlets, spinach, yogurt, and whole-wheat bread set aside their plain, wholesome image and assume a more elegant demeanor. Easy faux pastry and a cool, minty filling hold together, and hold up, even in warm weather.

*t*oast Cups: Cut crusts from bread and roll bread flat with a rolling pin. Cut slices into quarters. Press into lightly oiled miniature muffin pans. Bake in a preheated 350° oven for about 10 minutes, or until cups just begin to crisp. Let cool. □ The cups are best filled just before serving, but they will hold 1 to 2 hours without getting soggy. Garnish each cup with a mint sprig. □ Makes about 80 mini cups.

Filling: In a large sauté pan heat oil and sauté onions until translucent. Add spinach and mix well. Cook until heated through. Let cool.□ Combine yogurt, garlic, mint, salt and pepper, and walnuts. Add to spinach mixture. Cover and chill.

TOAST CUPS:

1 loaf thin-sliced whole-wheat bread

FILLING:

¼ cup safflower oil

1 medium onion, minced

Two 10-ounce packages frozen chopped spinach, thawed and well drained

1¼ cups plain yogurt

1 garlic clove, minced

2 tablespoons minced fresh mint

Dash salt

Dash ground black pepper

3 tablespoons walnuts, chopped and toasted

GARNISH:

Mint sprigs

118

*t*rim crusts from bread and cut bread into 2½-inch equilateral triangles. Cover. □ Cut salmon and cucumber into ½-inch wide strips. Cut unseeded cucumber lengthwise. □ Spread triangles with cream cheese. Arrange alternating bands of salmon and cucumber over cheese. Trim ends. Garnish with mustard, herbs, and lemon zest. Serve. □ *Note:* To save time, you can prepare squares in the same manner and cut in half on the diagonal. The result will simply be right angle rather than equilateral triangles. □ Makes 12 canapes.

12 thin slices rye bread, 6 light, 6 black

12 slices smoked salmon

1 English cucumber, peeled and cut into 2½-inch segments

4 ounces whipped cream cheese

Sweet prepared mustard

Assorted herb sprigs

Lemon zest

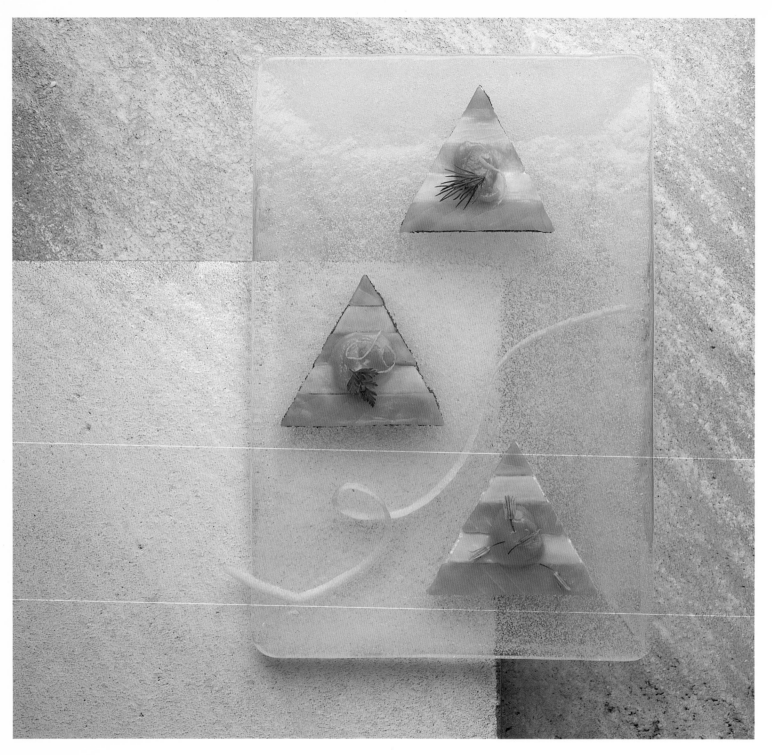

This is a smoked-salmon and cucumber hors d'oeuvre of a different stripe. The main ingredients are a classic combination, but the geometric presentation provides an intriguing perspective for applying a range of garnitures, from a refreshing slice of lemon to a pungent dollop of sweet honey mustard.

Sold by the gram—not the kar-
at, as might befit its pre-
cious standing—caviar
is the perfect finger
food, to be enjoyed in
small portions due to its
specialness and cost. Beluga is
the largest-grained and most ex-
pensive, although Ossetra and Sevruga,
also from the Caspian Sea sturgeon, are ex-
cellent as well. Newer varieties of these "slightly salted pearls" come from the Chinese sturgeon,
and bright orange Tobiko—roe from the flying fish,
barely bigger than poppy seed—is commonly used in sushi
restaurants for its light fish flavor and crunchy texture.

*e*nglish Cucumber Canapes: Slice a disc of cucumber ¼ inch thick for each canape base. Slice 5 paper-thin cucumber half-rounds and fan them out over base. Dot with sour cream and caviar. Top with chives.

Rose Petal Toasts with Beluga: Top each toast square with 2 rose petals, a dollop of sour cream, and a dollop of Beluga caviar.

Omelette Cones with Tobiko: In a small non-stick omelette pan, melt butter. Add one-fourth of beaten egg, to form a 4-inch omelette. Cook over medium-low heat until egg begins to set. Using a rubber spatula, lift edges to allow uncooked egg to run under omelette. When set, turn onto waxed paper. Repeat process to make 4 omelettes. Slice cooled omelettes in half. Roll into cones and fill with sour cream and caviar. Garnish with a chive wand. □ Makes 8 cones.

ENGLISH CUCUMBER CANAPES:

1 English cucumber

Sour cream or crème fraîche

Golden caviar

Chives cut into ¼-inch pieces

ROSE PETAL TOASTS:

Thin slices white bread, trimmed of crusts, cut into 1½-inch squares, and toasted

Garden rose petals (pesticide free)

Sour cream or crème fraîche

Beluga caviar

OMELETTE CONES:

Unsalted butter for frying

2 eggs beaten with 1 tablespoon water

Sour cream or crème fraîche

Tobiko caviar

Chives

GARNISH:

Sprig of salad burnet

*h*eat oil in a covered saucepan or popcorn maker and pop corn according to package directions. Toss popcorn with olives and raisins. □ Melt butter. Add Italian herbs. Drizzle over popcorn mixture. □ Serves 4.

3 tablespoons oil

½ cup unpopped popcorn

24 dry-cured black olives, pitted and halved

⅓ cup raisins, plumped

2 tablespoons salted butter

¼ teaspoon mixed dried Italian herbs

Popcorn is a seed
that heat turns in-
side out; at about
400° the puffed white
interior is released in a tiny
explosion. Beloved with just a drizzle of
butter and a shake of salt, popcorn takes
easily to a variety of seasonings. This
unexpected combination of sweet and spicy is
not simply a curiosity—it is delicious with cock-
tails, and not greasy, either.

French toast steps from the breakfast counter to the buffet table as a savory open-faced sandwich. Fried in a golden coating of exotic saffron batter, slices of stale baguette serve as the base for elegant mix-and-match compositions.

*a*llow baguette slices to sit in open air to dry. ☐ In a shallow container, beat together eggs and milk. Add saffron. Let stand 45 minutes. ☐ Soak slices of bread in egg mixture. Let excess batter drain off. ☐ Fry on a greased griddle or in a skillet about 3 minutes per side, turning once. ☐ Top each slice with a dollop of sour cream and chutney and a slice of kumquat. Serve warm. ☐ Makes 12 to 15 slices.

1 day-old baguette sliced diagonally into ½-inch thick ovals

3 eggs

¾ cup milk

½ teaspoon saffron threads

Butter for frying

¼ cup sour cream, drained on paper towels

Spicy tomato chutney or other chutney of choice

Kumquats cut into thin slices

*S*pread toast with a thin layer of peanut butter. □ Select cookie cutters in simple shapes and press out canapes. (Cutters with intricate forms will clog and tear.) □ Top each canape with a piece of fresh fruit.

Thin-sliced whole-wheat bread, toasted

Unsalted smooth peanut butter

Assorted fruit, cut into bite-sized shapes

When food devotees get together and cook, their kids may eye the results and ask, "What's to eat?" These "canapes with training wheels" offer familiar, kid-friendly—and healthful—ingredients, prepared and presented like fancy party food. Youngsters may even be inspired to take up the cookie cutters themselves.

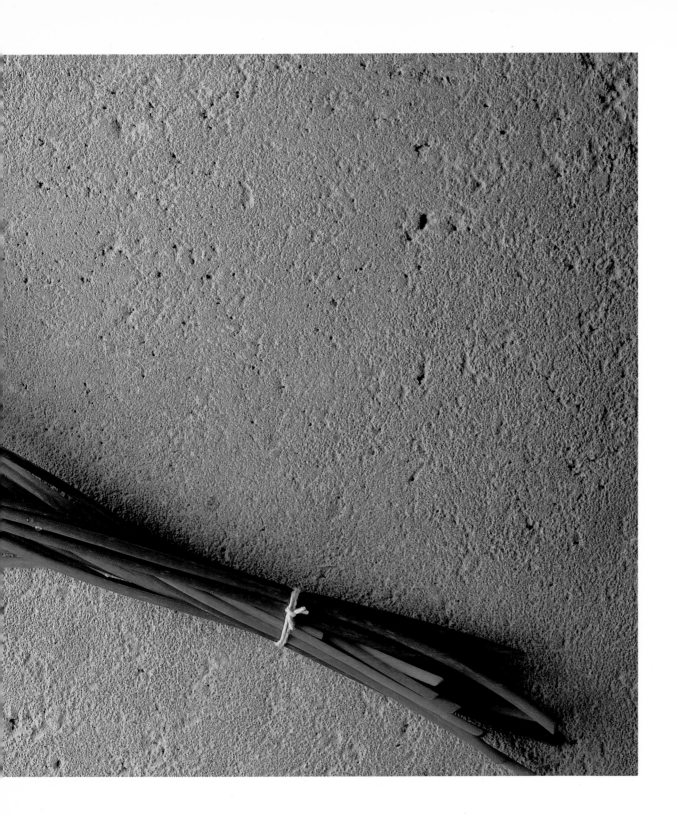

BIBLIOGRAPHY

Brennan, Georgeanne; Cronin, Isaac; & Glenn, Charlotte.
The New American Vegetable Cookbook.
Berkeley, Ca.:
Aris Books,
1985.

Conran, Terence and Caroline.
Conran Cookbook: The Purchase and
Preparation of Food.
New York:
Weathervane Books,
1986.

Hazan, Marcella.
The Classic Italian Cook Book.
New York:
Alfred A. Knopf,
1983.

Ortho Editorial Staff and McNair, James K.
The World of Herbs and Spices.
San Francisco:
Ortho Books,
1978.

Root, Waverley.
Food.
New York:
Simon & Schuster,
1980.

Schneider, Elizabeth.
Uncommon Fruits and Vegetables: A Commonsense Guide.
New York:
Harper & Row,
1986.

Time-Life Books Editorial Staff.
Vegetables,
The Good Cook/Techniques and Recipes Series.
Alexandria, Va.:
Time-Life Books,
1979.

INDEX